Real HEROES EAT HAMBURGERS

5-Minute Devotions for Kids

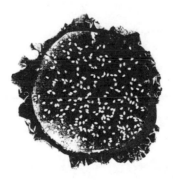

by Tim Hansel

Chariot Books™
David C. Cook Publishing Co.

Published by Chariot Books™,
an imprint of David C. Cook Publishing Co.
David C. Cook Publishing Co., Elgin, Illinois 60120
David C. Cook Publishing Co., Weston, Ontario

REAL HEROES EAT HAMBURGERS
© 1989 by Tim Hansel

Unless otherwise noted, all Scripture quotations in this publication are from the Holy Bible, New International Version. Copyright © 1973, 1978, 1984, International Bible Society.

Verses marked (TLB) are taken from *The Living Bible* © 1971, owned by assignment by Illinois Regional Bank N.A. (as trustee). Used by permission of Tyndale House Publishers Inc., Wheaton, IL 60189. All rights reserved.

Cover and interior design by Elizabeth Thompson.
Illustrations by Joe Van Severen.

First Printing, 1989
Printed in the United States of America
93 92 91 90 89 5 4 3 2 1

Library of Congress Cataloging-in-Publication Data

Hansel, Tim.
  Real heroes eat hamburgers.

  Summary: Presents a collection of anecdotes, prayers, and Bible verses focusing on developing courage to face difficult situations in life.
  1. Children—Prayer-books and devotions—English. [1. Prayer books and devotions] 1. Van Severen, Joe, ill. II. Title.
BV4870.H25   1989   242'.62   89-9952
ISBN 1-55513-334-7

TABLE OF
CONTENTS

STOP!
Read this first.

Have you ever wanted to be a hero...or at least brave enough to do what none of your friends dared to do? If you were a hero, people might use words like brave, gutsy, daring, courageous, and fearless, to describe you.

Some kids think heroes are only in comic books or maybe playing football for the 49ers, or making lots of money in a rock band. But real heroes are people like the friends you'll meet in this book. And when you've thought about it, I think you'll see how you can be a hero, too. That's why I've written this book. The world needs young people who know how to live like heroes. I hope you will be one of those young people who is willing to go on a real hero adventure.

Tim Hansel

HERO PRACTICE:

Some kids might say, "I don't know how I could ever be a hero." The section marked "Hero Practice" will help you find out what it feels like for you to be a *real* hero.

TAKE COURAGE:

God's Word is full of words of courage. When you see "Take Courage," a Bible verse will give you courage to be the hero God wants you to be.

PRAYER:

Sometimes it's difficult to pray. You want to say something to God, but don't know where to start. The prayers in this book will help you get started. Then you can add whatever you want to say to God.

ANSWER CHECK:

Make a check in the box when your prayer is answered. One of the best ways to build up your courage is to look back through the book and see how many prayers God has already answered.

Your words are important!

We've left you extra room throughout this book so you can write or draw your thoughts and ideas. Have fun!

About Tim Hansel...

Tim Hansel has done things most of us only dream about. He's sailed 25,000 miles on the Pacific Ocean in a forty-three-foot boat. He's climbed one of the highest mountains in the United States. He's worked with some of the toughest gangs in New York City, helping gang members get to know Jesus Christ.

After coaching high school soccer and college football, Tim started Summit Expedition, an organization that takes kids and adults on wilderness and mountain-climbing trips. One of the most exciting Summit programs is GO FOR IT, especially for handicapped people.

It's a Horse, Of Course

Bo Nixon and I had just arrived at the Young Life Colorado ranch with a load of kids from New York's inner city. One of the kids was Mike, whose gang name was "Hatchet Man." (Bo said, "because that's his favorite weapon.")

Mike pointed to an animal standing nearby and said, "Hey, what's that?"

"It's a horse," we told him, surprised that he didn't know.

"Naw, that's no horse," Mike said. "Horses ain't that big because I've seen 'em on TV and they're just little teeny things!"

Mike may not know much about horses, but that week at Young Life camp he became a real hero. That's because he had the courage to let Jesus Christ change his life from a tough New York City gang member to a person who decided to live for God.

HERO PRACTICE:

You may not live in a rough neighborhood, but it may still be hard for you to live for God where you are. Remember that God is with you as you think about living for Him this week.

TAKE COURAGE:

"The Lord is my light and my salvation—whom shall I fear? The Lord is the stronghold of my life—of whom shall I be afraid?"   Psalm 27:1

PRAYER:

Give me courage, Lord, to live for You this week.

ANSWER CHECK:

Real heroes...
have courage to live for Christ.

The Heart of King Kong

I first met Sherry Leonard when she was a counselor at Young Life camp. And I wondered, how did this frail-looking girl who can't even walk get to be so happy? It was as though life just giggled and danced inside her. She had a heart as big as King Kong. Teenagers loved her because they could tell she loved them. And because she felt so good about herself, she made them feel good about themselves.

I found out that Sherry was nine when she began losing her muscle power. She had muscular dystrophy, an illness that paralyzes your muscles. For a few years she was discouraged because she couldn't get around like other people. She even asked God to help her die. Then she realized that God doesn't make mistakes.

Now she says, "Muscular dystrophy is my gift from God. It has made it easier to tell people about Jesus Christ." Sherry has learned to relax and leave her life in God's hands, because she knows that God can turn even muscular dystrophy into something good.

HERO PRACTICE:

If God can turn a handicap like Sherry's into something good, what problem of yours could you leave in God's hands?

TAKE COURAGE:

"Be delighted with the Lord. Then he will give you all your heart's desires. Commit everything you do to the Lord. Trust him to help you do it and he will."

Psalm 37:4, 5, TLB

PRAYER:

You know how big my problems seem to me, Lord. Thank You for being bigger than any of them. One problem that I would like to give to You is:

ANSWER CHECK:

Real heroes. . .
trust God with their problems.

Blood Brothers

The first time I ate rattlesnake meat was with my friend Shelton Chow at his mom's restaurant. We had decided early on to be "blood brothers." So Shelton invited me to the special "family only" dinner at the restaurant, even though that made me the only person there who wasn't Chinese.

Shelton is on my list of real heroes because he was color-blind. Oh, there was nothing wrong with his eyes. He just refused to make a big deal about whether someone was white or black or brown or whatever. He even invited me to play in his all-Chinese basketball league. "This is my blood brother," he said when he introduced me to the group. So they let me play the whole season because of Shelton.

Shelton looked at people the way God does. What's really important isn't the color of our skin, but what we are like on the inside.

HERO PRACTICE:

Do you know some kids who look different than you do? Do you treat them the same as kids who are more like you? What would you need to do to be a hero to those kids who look different than you?

TAKE COURAGE:

". . .we are all the same. . .we are one in Christ Jesus." Galatians 3:28b, TLB

PRAYER:

It's easy to forget, God, that You see us from the inside out. Help me to look at all the kids with eyes that are "color-blind."

ANSWER CHECK:

Real heroes...
are "color blind."

Oh, Wow!

I hated to think about climbing out of my warm and toasty sleeping bag even though it looked like the start of a beautiful day in the Sierra Mountains. Because I once broke my back in a mountain-climbing accident, it's always hard to move in the morning. So, I was kind of feeling sorry for myself that morning until I looked over and saw Tim Burton begin to struggle out of his sleeping bag.

Tim was a carpenter. One day he fell off a wooden construction platform and hit his head. Since that time he has not been able to walk, and has trouble moving and even talking. Now he was working as hard as he could to get out of that sleeping bag by himself. It took him half an hour! But he kept at it, and when he was finally out, he looked over at me and said in his stammering voice, "Ok-k-kay, Tim. I'm r-r-ready f-for a-a-a-anything!"

Later, as he struggled up the side of the mountain with the help of two instructors, he kept saying, "Oh, W-W-Wow!" He was so thankful to be making the climb, even though it was hard. We named the climb "Oh, Wow" after Tim Burton.

HERO PRACTICE:

Think of something that's hard for you to do. Then think about Tim Burton. How can you be a hero about difficult things?

TAKE COURAGE:

"And we pray this in order that you may live a life worthy of the Lord and may please him in every way. . .that you may have great endurance and patience." Colossians 1:10, 11

PRAYER:

Thank You for always being there to help when something seems too hard for me. I love You, Jesus.

ANSWER CHECK:

Real heroes. . .
never quit trying.

No Ordinary Dentist

Dr. Ken Campbell is no ordinary dentist. For one thing, he doesn't look ordinary. He has no eyebrows, and the skin around his eyes and mouth is pulled back tight. That's because he was burned very badly in a car crash several years ago. He and his girlfriend were waiting at a stop sign when their car was hit by a huge tanker truck. The car burst into flames. Ken's girlfriend was killed. The burns were so painful that Ken prayed that he would die. But God had other plans for him, and that's another reason Ken isn't an ordinary dentist.

Ken decided to not give up, and to let God help him get well. Now he often talks to people about Jesus while he fixes their teeth. He tells people that the reason he's alive is because of Jesus Christ. Sometimes he takes trips to Central America where he gives free dental help to people who couldn't get it otherwise.

HERO PRACTICE:

Maybe you think that if you were just a little older, or a little smarter, or if you knew the "right words," you could be a witness for Jesus. This week, remember how God helped Dr. Ken be a witness for Him, even when he thought his life was over, and then see how God can help you.

TAKE COURAGE:

"I tell you, whoever acknowledges me before men, the Son of Man will also acknowledge him before the angels of God."   Luke 12:8

PRAYER:

Sometimes I don't want to say anything about You, God, especially to kids who might laugh. Help me to be a witness for You even when I'm afraid.

ANSWER CHECK:

Real heroes . . .
live for Jesus right
where they are.

Rich Guy from Pittsburgh

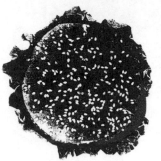

Bill Milliken didn't know what he was getting into when he rode into a New York inner city ghetto ready to help. The kids he met there were tough and not sure they wanted any help from this Christian guy from Pittsburgh. Many of them were members of street gangs. They were used to living with fighting on the streets and at home.

Bill discovered one of the real meanings of *hero* –"a person who tries to help others no matter what happens." He kept on trying to learn how to do this, even though it was dangerous and discouraging. And many of the kids became Christians and changed their ways. One of them, Bo Nixon, president of the Young Pagans gang, now directs a ministry to street kids in New York City.

HERO PRACTICE:

You don't have to go to a New York City ghetto to be a real hero. Look around your own neighborhood and see what you could do to help right now.

TAKE COURAGE:

"The Lord himself goes before you and will be with you; he will never leave you nor forsake you. Do not be afraid; do not be discouraged."

Deuteronomy 31:8

PRAYER:

Lord, please help me to see what I can do to be a real hero in my neighborhood.

ANSWER CHECK:

Real heroes. . .
try to help others no matter what happens.

Try, Try Again

It takes a lot of courage to try something again when you think you've never been good at it. Pam had never liked school. She considered herself a poor student. When she managed to get through high school and a little bit of college she decided that was enough. It was just too hard.

But after she was married and her kids got older, she realized that she would have to go back to college to get the job she wanted. She was scared. But Pam knew it was worth trying again. Now she's glad she did because she was not only able to graduate from college, but then went on to get her master's degree to become a psychologist. This was something she had always wanted to do. Pam is a very important hero to me because she is my wife.

HERO PRACTICE:

Think of something you wish you didn't have to try to do again. It's just too hard. How can you have courage to try again?

TAKE COURAGE:

"I have set the Lord always before me. Because he is at my right hand, I will not be shaken."

Psalm 16:8

PRAYER:

Dear God, it's just too hard for me to _____
_____.
Please give me the courage to try again. Thank You.

ANSWER CHECK:

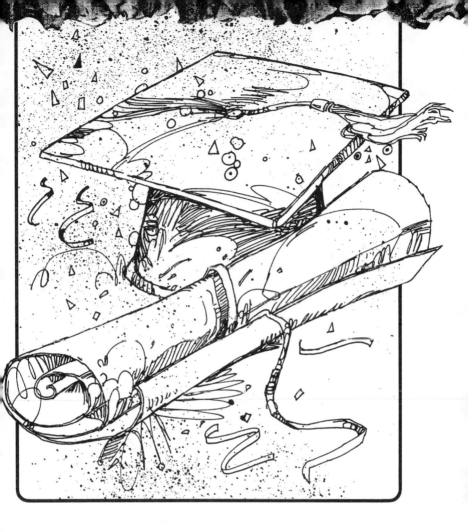

Real heroes...
keep going even when they feel like giving up.

Joy

It's five in the morning. The sun is barely up and you can hardly see the football field. But Coach Parks is already here ready to run his fifty-five miles. Fifty-five miles! Well, let me explain.

Every year on his birthday, the coach celebrates by running the years of his age in miles around the football field. Today, he's fifty-five, and it will take him all day. And all day he'll have kids out there running with him.

Why would he do this? I mean, fifty-five is old!

He's doing it to raise money for the poor in Africa. He has people pledge a certain amount per mile. You see, Coach Parks has discovered one of the meanings of joy: *J*esus first, *O*thers next, and then *Y*ourself. He knows he is happiest when he's doing something for other people.

HERO PRACTICE:

Think of a time when you did something for a person in your family or for a friend. How did you feel? You were probably feeling joy the way Coach Parks spells it — *J-O-Y*.

TAKE COURAGE:

"The joy of the Lord is your strength."

Nehemiah 8:10

 ## PRAYER:

Feeling joy is great, Lord. I want to remember to live for You today with *J-O-Y.*

 # ANSWER CHECK:

Real heroes. . .

find joy in helping others.

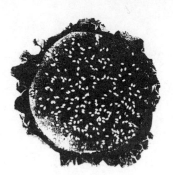

Giant on the Inside

I know a guy who is probably only four feet tall, but inside he's a real giant. Zane Mills has a problem with his nervous system that makes even ordinary things like brushing teeth and turning off the TV big and difficult. He can't walk and sometimes has a hard time just breathing, but he doesn't let that slow him down.

But Zane decided a long time ago that he would try as hard as he could to do everything well. Even though he couldn't finish his college work to become a doctor like he first wanted, he became a high school teacher in science and math. And he learned to drive a specially equipped car so he could get around by himself.

Everyone knows Zane as a loving, caring person. People hardly notice his small frame because his life shows that he's a giant on the inside—where it really counts.

HERO PRACTICE:

You might feel a lot like Zane Mills when you think you're not tall enough or old enough or good enough at doing something. Take a minute to name the things you *can* do. What are you good at? When have you felt really good about yourself?

TAKE COURAGE:

"However, Christ has given each of us special abilities—whatever he wants us to have out of his rich storehouse of gifts." Ephesians 4:7, TLB

PRAYER:

Thank You, God, for me. Thank You for making me just the way I am. Thank You for loving me just the way I am.

ANSWER CHECK:

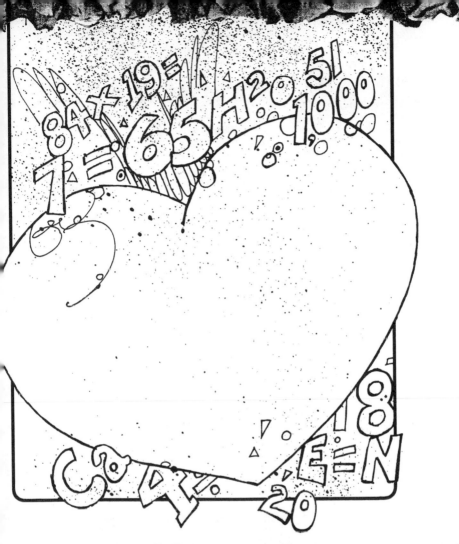

Real heroes. . .
are learning to use the special gifts God gives them.

French Fries and Hamburgers

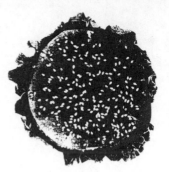

Could you draw a picture of a horse with your toes? Or could you eat french fries and hamburgers with your feet?

One day my friend Anna, who's nine, and her father took me to lunch at Wendy's. When I started eating my baked potato, I noticed some toes reaching up to the table, picking up french fries. You see, Anna was born without arms, so she has learned to eat with her feet. You should see her devour a hamburger!

With a lot of practice (and God's help) Anna has learned to use her feet the way you and I use our hands. One of her favorite things is drawing pictures of horses. She also helps her father in his business.

"Anna is my catalog maker," her father told me. With her feet she arranges the loose pages in order before they are stapled. For Anna, difficulties are just challenges she meets every day.

HERO PRACTICE:

What is the toughest thing you have to do this week? Take a minute to think of what that might be. Remember you can do it with God's help.

TAKE COURAGE:

"I can do everything through him who gives me strength." Philippians 4:13

PRAYER:

I know that You are with me this week, God. One thing I need help with is:

ANSWER CHECK:

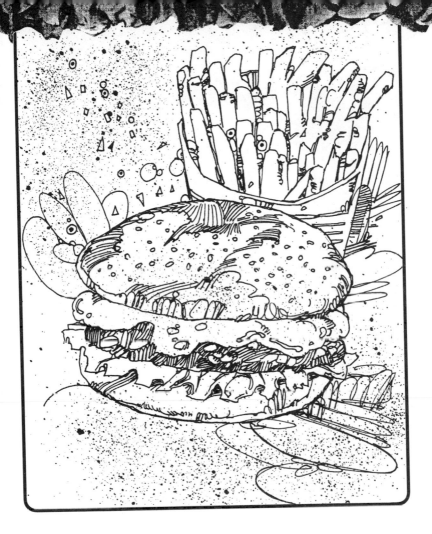

Real heroes. . .

can do anything they need to do with God's help.

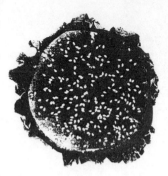

When You're the Only One

Have you noticed that in almost every class there is one kid who gets picked on? In a class that my son Josh was in, everyone teased a girl who couldn't do things as well as other kids could—like running and catching a ball. Josh went along with the mean teasing at first, until one day when he started thinking about how the girl must feel.

Now Josh has stopped teasing her, and that's one reason he's a hero. It takes courage to stand up for what you know is right, especially when you're the only one who will.

HERO PRACTICE:

Next time you're tempted to tease someone in a mean way, remember how you felt when it happened to you. Ask God to help you act kindly, even if you are the only one who does.

TAKE COURAGE:

"Be kind and compassionate to one another."

Ephesians 4:32

 # PRAYER:

Help me remember, God, how mean teasing feels
when I am tempted to do it this week.

 ANSWER CHECK:

Real heroes...
stand up for what they
know is right, even
when they're the only
ones who do.

49

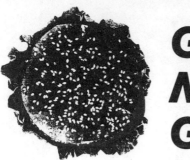

Good Morning, God

Don McClean is a great fisherman. Sometimes I think he could catch his limit in a bathtub!

We went backpacking together in the Sierras one summer. When I heard him up making coffee early in the morning, I just rolled over and tried to go back to sleep. But Don was over there roaring with laughter, trying to think up ways to get me out of my sleeping bag. "I'm going to throw you in the river if you don't get out of bed," he laughed.

Groaning, I rolled out. I thought he wanted to go fishing. But Don wanted me to get up and join him for a "good morning" time with God. He believes God is the most important person in his life, and he wants to talk to God and listen to Him first every morning.

Later we did go fishing. As usual, Don caught his limit and I caught two skinny ones.

HERO PRACTICE:

Sometimes it's hard to talk to someone you can't see or hear. That's why it's important to try to make a special time each day when you can get quiet and talk to God. When is the best time in your day for you to talk to God? Where? How can you hear God talk to you?

TAKE COURAGE:

"Be still, and know that I am God." Psalm 46:10

PRAYER:

I need to talk to You, God. And I need to hear what You have to say to me. Thank You for the Bible and for speaking to me through Your words there.

ANSWER CHECK:

Real heroes. . .
take time to get quiet and talk to God.

One Small Step

I was in the Los Angeles airport with my sons, Josh and Zac, when I spotted Bob Wieland in a crowd of travelers. "C'mon guys," I said, "this is someone you have to meet."

It's not every day that you get to meet someone who has walked across America. And Bob Wieland did it on his hands! Bob was a six-foot, 205-pound, medical corpsman in Viet Nam when he stepped on a hidden bomb that blew off both his legs. When Bob recovered from the accident he began training, lifting weights to strengthen his body. At first he could only lift five pounds. Today he can lift over 500 pounds in the bench press! It took him 4.9 million "steps" to walk across America, swinging his body along on his hands, wearing thickly padded gloves. He started at Knotts Berry Farm in California on September 8, 1982, and ended up at the Viet Nam War Memorial in Washington D.C. three years, eight months, and six days later! Why did he do it? "To encourage those with legs to take the first step in faith to please God."

Bob knows that when you do that, you are a hero no matter what happens.

HERO PRACTICE:

Bob Wieland started out small when he began lifting weights—only five pounds. You can begin living to please God by doing a very small thing. Where could you start? What could be your "first step"?

TAKE COURAGE:

"Whoever can be trusted with very little can also be trusted with much." Luke 16:10

 # PRAYER:

I want to please You, God. One small way I can try to please You is:

ANSWER CHECK:

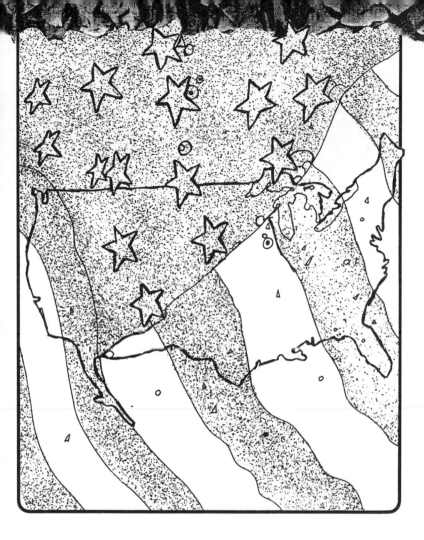

Real heroes . . .
want to please God even in small ways.

My First Real Hero

It was one of those perfect spring days. My older brother, Steve, and I were playing baseball with some kids up at Volunteer Park. As usual, Steve let me tag along with him and his friends. He was that kind of guy.

I was pitching when one of the kids hit a line drive in my direction. I held out my glove to catch the ball, but instead it hit me right between the eyes and knocked me unconscious. As my fuzzy, aching head cleared, I heard a man running across the field hollering, "Can I help you?"

And then my brother was there, stooping in the dirt, helping me up and saying, "No, I can take care of it. This happens every spring."

It was true. I was always cracking my head open or something, and Steve was always there to help. I guess he was my first real hero—the kind of brother everyone wishes they had, cheering for me, encouraging me, and putting up with me no matter what I did. I can still remember what he always said to me, "Way to go, Bro!"

HERO PRACTICE:

Do you have a brother or sister? How could you be a "hero" to him or her? If you don't have a brother or sister, whom do you know who needs one? Could you volunteer?

TAKE COURAGE:

"Therefore encourage one another and build each other up, just as in fact you are doing."

I Thessalonians 5:11

PRAYER:

Thank You, God, for brothers and sisters, and for some friends who are like brothers or sisters to me. Help me be a hero to them in some way.

ANSWER CHECK:

Real heroes . . .

are learning to be a real "brother" or "sister."

Do you know any *real heroes*? In what ways have you been a real hero since reading this book? When is it most difficult for you to be a real hero?

Tim Hansel would like to hear your answers to these questions. You can write to him at:

Tim Hansel
c/o Chariot Books
850 N. Grove Ave.
Elgin, IL 60120

September 30, 1990

Emily,

It has been really fun having you in our childrens church. We have watched you grow from a shy little girl who wouldn't answer any questions to the little lady you are now who has most all the answers. We are proud of you. This book is to help you to continue to grow in Christ. Joyce, Kevin and I hope that we have shared something with you that you can now go into the regular church and share with others.

We Love You

Laurie